Survivors of the Holocaust

Jane Shuter

Heinemann Library
Chicago, Illinois

Designed by Joanna Sapwell and Tinstar Design
Illustrations by Martin Griffin
Originated by Ambassador Litho Ltd
Printed in China, by Wing King Tong

07 06 05 04 03
10 9 8 7 6 5 4 3 2 1

**Library of Congress
Cataloging-in-Publication Data**
Shuter, Jane.
   Survivors of the Holocaust / Jane Shuter.
      p. cm. -- (The Holocaust)
   Includes bibliographical references and index.
Summary: Tells the stories of some people who managed to survive the Holocaust and how they did it.
   ISBN 1-4034 0810-6 (HC) 1-4034-3202-3 (Pbk.)
   1. Holocaust, Jewish (1939-1945)--Personal narratives--Juve-nile literature. 2. Holocaust survivors--Biography--Juvenile literature. [1. Holocaust survivors. 2. Holocaust, Jewish (1939-1945)]   I. Title. II. Series: Holocaust (Chicago, Ill.)
   D804.34.S74 2002
   940.53'18'0922--d
                           2002006852

Acknowledgments
The author and publisher are grateful to the following for permission to reproduce copyright material: pp. 4, 10, 13, 20, 24, 34, 36, 37, 41, 43, 46, 47, 49 USHMM; p. 6 Art Archive/National Archives; pp. 8, 9 Anne Fox/Vallentine Mitchell; pp. 11, 18, 21 Gerda Weissmann Klein; pp. 12, 14, 15 Houghton Mifflin; p. 16 Rich Cohen; p. 17 Popperfoto; pp. 22, 25, 31, 35 Auschwitz-Birkenau State Museum; pp. 23, 30, 33 Emma Robertson/Magnet Harlequin; pp. 26, 27 Estate of Hugo Gryn; p. 28 Leiberose Archive; p. 29 Naomi Gryn; p. 32 Weiner Library; p. 38 AKG; p. 39 Eva Panas; p. 40 Rudolf Vrba; p. 42 Yad Vashem; pp. 44, 45 Leon Greenman; p. 48 Hulton Archive

Cover photograph reproduced with the permission of Hulton Archive.

Special thanks to Ronald Smelser and Sally Brown-Winter.

About the series consultants
Ronald Smelser is a history professor at the University of Utah. He has written or edited eight books on the Holocaust and Nazi Germany and over three dozen articles. His recent publications include *Learning About the Holocaust: A Student Guide* (4 vol.) and *Lessons and Legacies: The Holocaust and Justice*. Professor Smelser is also a past president of the German Studies Association.

Sally Brown-Winter has worked in the field of Jewish Education as a principal and teacher for over 25 years. In her schools, the Shoah—its history, lessons, and implications—have been explored from kindergarten through high school.

Some words are shown in bold, **like this.** You can find out what they mean by looking in the glossary.

Contents

The Nazis and the Holocaust 4

Getting Out Early 8

Going into Hiding 12

Surviving the Camps 18

Surviving by Cooperating 32

Surviving by Escaping .38

Different Chances 42

A Closer Look: Feelings About Survival 46

Timeline 50

Glossary 52

Further Reading 54

Places of Interest and Websites 55

Index 56

The Nazis and the Holocaust

In 1933 the **Nazi** Party, led by Adolf Hitler, came to power in Germany. It wanted to create a new German empire, the **Third Reich.** This new empire would be far bigger than Germany, so the Nazis began to plan how to take over other countries. They also believed that the Germans were superior to all other **races,** so they began to discriminate against anyone who did not fit their idea of a perfect German.

Czech Political Prisoners

When Germany invaded Czechoslovakia in 1939, many Czechs fought back. Those who were caught, like the men in this photo, were sent to the camps.

The Camp System

The Nazis arrested people they saw as political opponents and put them in special prison camps. These were different from ordinary prisons because camp prisoners were not given a trial and had no date for their release. They lived and worked in appalling conditions and they died, or were killed, in large numbers. The first of these camps, Dachau, was set up just four days after the Nazis won power in the March 1933 election.

The camps were run by the **SS** (short for *Schutzstaffel*—security staff), which had been set up as Hitler's private bodyguard. They all swore an oath of loyalty to Hitler, not Germany. The SS grew to take over parts of the army and to run the camp system. The camps were very effective. By 1935, very few Germans openly opposed the Nazis. So, instead of political opponents, the Nazis filled the camps with people they considered **undesirable**— people such as drunks, criminals, the unemployed, Jehovah's Witnesses, and those who the Nazis saw as belonging to "inferior races." The Nazis had very firm, but very wrong ideas about race. They invented a race, a group of people with the same ancestors far in the past, called **Aryans.** According to the Nazis, these people had pure German blood and were superior to all other people. The Nazis thought that Aryans could take what they wanted and do what they liked to people from other "inferior" racial groups.

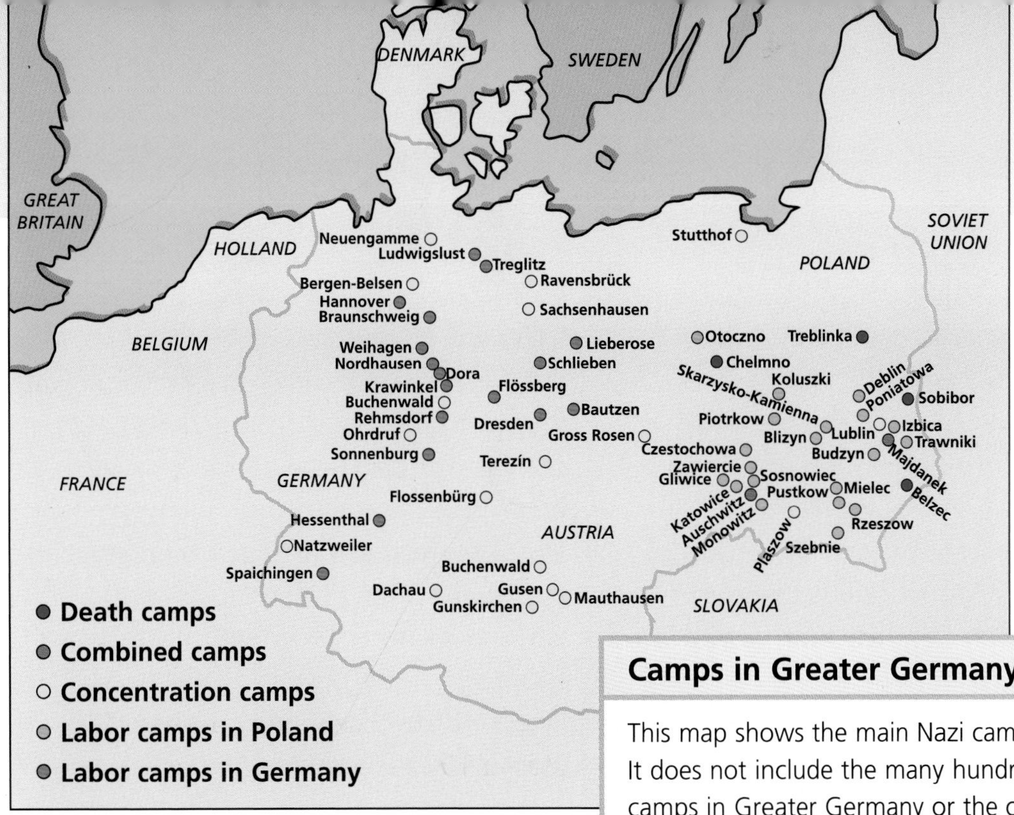
DENMARK
SWEDEN
GREAT BRITAIN
HOLLAND
BELGIUM
FRANCE
GERMANY
AUSTRIA
POLAND
SOVIET UNION
SLOVAKIA
Neuengamme
Ludwigslust
Treglitz
Ravensbrück
Bergen-Belsen
Hannover
Braunschweig
Sachsenhausen
Stutthof
Weihagen
Nordhausen
Dora
Krawinkel
Buchenwald
Rehmsdorf
Ohrdruf
Sonnenburg
Lieberose
Schlieben
Flössberg
Dresden
Bautzen
Gross Rosen
Terezín
Flossenbürg
Hessenthal
Natzweiler
Spaichingen
Buchenwald
Dachau
Gusen
Gunskirchen
Mauthausen
Otoczno
Treblinka
Chelmno
Koluszki
Skarzysko-Kamienna
Piotrkow
Deblin
Poniatowa
Sobibor
Izbica
Trawniki
Lublin
Blizyn
Budzyn
Majdanek
Czestochowa
Zawiercie
Gliwice
Sosnowiec
Pustkow
Mielec
Belzec
Katowice
Auschwitz
Monowitz
Plaszow
Rzeszow
Szebnie
Death camps
Combined camps
Concentration camps
Labor camps in Poland
Labor camps in Germany

Camps in Greater Germany

This map shows the main Nazi camps in 1942. It does not include the many hundreds of small camps in Greater Germany or the camps in other countries **occupied** by the Germans.

The Nazi Empire

The Nazis began to build their empire by taking over other countries. In 1938 they took over Austria and part of Czechoslovakia. In 1939 they invaded the rest of Czechoslovakia and, later, Poland. Britain and France eventually reacted to the invasion of Poland by declaring war on Germany on September 3, 1939. By this point the German army was taking over more and more land. The Nazis made people in all of these lands obey Nazi laws. Their opponents in these countries were also put into the camps.

The Holocaust

The camps played a large part in the **Holocaust**—the deliberate attempt by the Nazis to kill all **Jewish** people in the lands they controlled. The Nazis used the first camps as prison camps for political prisoners. Many of these prisoners were Jewish, but they were imprisoned for their political beliefs, not for being Jewish. Many people died from the harsh conditions in these early camps. However, even when the Nazis found that they had broken down most political opposition, they did not close the camps. Instead, they expanded the camp system.

The Nazis filled the camps with those people who did not fit into their Nazi state or who came from racial groups that the Nazis believed were inferior to the Aryan racial group. People belonging to these racial groups, such as **Gypsies** and Jews, were given the worst jobs in the camps and died by the thousands from the harsh treatment. The Nazis decided they were not dying fast enough, though. They wanted to kill all of the Jewish people in the lands they controlled. Thus, they set up special camps, **death camps,** just to murder thousands of Jewish people each day.

Survivors

Millions of people died in the **Holocaust**—many historians estimate about 5.7 million **Jews** alone. Very few people who were sent to the **camps** survived. Often only one member of a large family survived, although some people were lucky enough to find a close relative who had survived. At first, the survivors were not encouraged to talk about their experiences. No matter where they set up home after the war, people's first reaction was something like: "It's over now, you were lucky, put it behind you and make a new life."

As time passed, people were more willing to listen to the survivors' stories, but some found it difficult to believe that they were telling the truth. However, the survivors, many of them young people, had much more complicated reactions. They wanted to forget, but they could not. What had happened was real; they had lived through it; they had lost family and friends to it. They felt lucky to be alive, but they also felt guilty and unworthy. They had been treated like animals for so long that it took them a while to adjust to "real" life.

For them, the camps had been real life—it was the new lives they were just beginning that seemed unreal.

How Did They Survive?

Most survivors agree that, while there were things that people could do to improve chances of survival, most survived by luck or the will of a higher power. It helped to have the support of loved ones; it helped to have been young and healthy at the start. It helped to have confidence and a hope of survival. None of these things counted at all, though, if a person upset an **SS** guard, or ended up in a group controlled by a particularly cruel guard. Nor did they affect the work people were given, or even the camps individuals were sent to. That was pure luck.

A Survivor of Buchenwald

This survivor was photographed after the **liberation** of Buchenwald camp by the United States Army on April 11, 1945. The liberators tried to record as much of what they found as possible because they knew that people would find it hard to believe.

Some Survivors' Views on How They Survived

Primo Levi was an Italian Jew who became a famous writer:

The ones who adapted to everything survived. Most did not adapt, and died. Shoes, for example. They would throw two deliberately mismatched shoes at you. One with a high heel, one without. We had to make complicated exchanges to find two shoes that fit. Some feet swelled, rubbed against the shoe, and became infected. At the hospital, swollen feet were not treated—those who had swollen feet were sent to the gas chambers.

Tadeusz Sobolewicz was a Polish **partisan** fighter who was sent to Auschwitz:

The answer is very simple. Any one of those who were killed could have survived. I could have easily been one of those who died. All these factors contributed: strong will, stamina, the length of stay, food, health, the ability to get on with other prisoners, friendship, and the help of others. Some were saved by faith in God or by a deep conviction that they would survive.

Abba Kovner, a Jewish partisan, spoke to survivors just after the war ended:

Why do you think you survived? Because you are smarter than those who died? Because you are better? No. You survived for one reason: you were lucky.

Elie Cohen was a Jewish doctor who was in Westerbork camp in the Netherlands and in Auschwitz:

Hope was both very important and very unimportant. It could keep you going. Pessimists died fast. But it could not actually save you.

A former member of the female orchestra at Auschwitz, interviewed anonymously, said:

Being part of a group was vital. There was a good group spirit in the orchestra and people kept you going when you might have given up had you been alone. We hustled each other to stay alive, to stay on course, to stay disciplined.

A Sense of Worth

It was hard for many survivors to get used to not being seen as vermin, which is how the **Nazis** had treated them. Indeed, in some places, and the survivors mention Poland most often, some people were still influenced by Nazi **propaganda.** They blamed the Jews for the war and treated badly the survivors who tried to return home. Some survivors themselves had trouble in seeing themselves as "real people" at first. Gerda Weissmann Klein remembers her liberation:

The soldier jumped from the truck and greeted me. I must tell him, I thought, from the start. Remember, for six long years the Nazis had treated us like dirt. "May I see the other ladies?" he asked. He probably doesn't know, I thought. I must tell him. "We are Jews," I said in a small voice. "So am I," he answered.

Getting Out Early

The *Kindertransports*

Some **Jewish** people decided to leave Germany almost as soon as the **Nazis** took over. Sometimes it was impossible to get a whole family out, though. Many sent their children to safety. After a wave of Nazi brutality against Jews in 1938, Britain agreed to take 10,000 Jewish children, aged three months to seventeen years, without **visas,** just identity cards. The children needed to have homes to go to—either families or hostels set up by charity organizations. These rescue trips were known as ***Kindertransports.***

Anne Fox

Twelve-year-old Anne Fox left Berlin on a *Kindertransport* in December 1938. Her parents stayed behind in Berlin because they could not get visas. Anne's brother, Gunter, in England on a student visa, found a Jewish family to take Anne in:

> *Mrs. Pincus was kind, but she was not my mother, nor could her house replace our flat* [apartment] *with its central heating and other comforts. At school, there was another German **refugee** in my class and we were happy to be together, to speak our own language and laugh at the strange ways of the British.*

Evacuated

When war broke out in September 1939, Anne's school was evacuated to the countryside. She went to live on a farm in Swineshead, a small village in England. The village people were kind and welcoming and all of the children had been uprooted, so her position was not as odd. On Anne's fourteenth birthday her mother wrote: "I would have liked to bake a cake for you, but you will have to make do with this picture from a cookbook." Anne still has the picture. In February 1941 she went to a school run by and for refugees from Hitler's Germany.

Life in Cardiff

When Anne passed her exams at sixteen, she went to Cardiff, in Wales, to live with her brother and his wife, Connie. Her first job was with a dressmaker: "Miss Litchfield was supposed to train me, but left me in a room all day ripping seams and sewing hems." She only stayed a week. Connie found her a job in the local library.

London, 1938

This photo was taken when Anne arrived in London in December 1938.

The End of the War

When the war ended, Gunter contacted various organizations to try to find their parents. In September 1945, a letter arrived saying that Wilma Oppenheimer, a survivor now living in Denmark, remembered their mother from the camp at Terezín. They wrote to Wilma, who wrote back saying both parents had been in Terezín. Anne's father had died there. Her mother had been sent on a **transport** and had not contacted Wilma after the war. Wilma was sure she was dead. Anne says: "I did not grieve, I could not grieve. I had been a orphan for six years already and there was no funeral, no grave, no relatives left."

A New Life

Anne went on with life as before. Shortly after the end of the war she met Frank Fox, a Jewish-American soldier, at the library. They fell in love and got married in January 1946. Frank was sent home by the army in February, and Anne waited for her visa and other documents to arrive. When they came in May, she went to Southampton: "The ship waiting to take us to America was the *SS Washington*, the same ship that had brought me to England." Anne and Frank settled in the United States and had a family.

Swineshead Village School

A photo of the village school taken during the war. Anne is at the back on the far right.

Uncomfortable Survivor

Anne survived the **Holocaust.** She says that when she compares her war years with those of survivors trapped in Germany she feels uncomfortable being called a survivor. But she was separated from her parents at twelve, had to cope in a strange country, had to face finding out what had happened to her parents. When she went back to Germany with Frank: "I scanned the faces of the older people. Where were they when the Jews were being persecuted and gassed?"

She also visited Terezín, where her parents had been prisoners, and Auschwitz, where her mother was killed. "We, who were spared, must tell our children, so that they can tell their children what took place."

Fighting Back

Not all of the **Jews** who left Germany early were children. Jews of all ages emigrated from 1933 onward, in increasing numbers. Some were lucky enough to settle far away from the expanding borders of the German **Reich,** in countries that remained free throughout the war, such as the United States, Britain, and Palestine. Some Jews joined the armed forces of the country they had moved to, and some returned to Germany to fight. Fighting in the war was even more dangerous for them than it was for the other soldiers. If Jewish soldiers were captured and the **Nazis** discovered they were Jewish, they were sent to the camps, not treated as prisoners-of-war. Other Jews were smuggled back into **occupied** Germany to work with the **resistance** and **partisan** groups there. Others still, such as scientists and mathematicians, used their special skills against Germany from their new homes.

Kurt Klein

Kurt Klein was born in Walldorf, Germany, in 1920. When the Nazis came to power in 1933, Kurt's parents wanted to leave Germany. Like many families, they tried to get **visas** to emigrate. Kurt's sister left for the United States in 1936 and got a visa for Kurt in 1937. A year later, their brother joined them. Once one family member was in a country, it was easier to get another visa. It was a race against time to find the money and the various **papers** and visas they needed. During the *Kristallnacht* attacks of 1938, when the Nazis organized attacks on Jews across Germany, Kurt's parents were forced out of their home and their possessions were ransacked. In 1941 they were rounded up and sent to Gurs camp, in France. Their visas came through in 1942, but it was too late. Kurt's parents had been sent to Auschwitz.

Fighting in the U.S. Army

These Jewish soldiers fought in the U.S. Army. They were photographed near the U.S. camp at Aachen, Germany, in 1945.

Fighting the Nazis

When the United States joined the war in 1942, Kurt, as an American, was drafted into the army. He spoke good German, so he was made an intelligence officer. In 1945, Kurt was a lieutenant with the 5th Infantry, advancing through Czechoslovakia. His unit was busy **liberating camps,** rounding up Germans and questioning them. As a German speaker, Kurt was often needed in several interrogations at once. He remembers how the captured soldiers denied supporting the Nazis: "I thought I was fighting the Nazis. Yet I questioned many, many soldiers without finding one willing to admit to being a Nazi."

It was especially hard for him, as a Jew, to cope with what the Nazis had done to Jewish people. He had set off for Europe with the hope of finding his parents, but as the scale of the **Holocaust** became clear to him, that hope faded.

Kurt Klein

This photo of Kurt Klein was taken in 1945, the year the war ended.

Building a Future

One of the **labor camps** the 5th Infantry liberated, in May 1945, was Volary camp, where Kurt met Gerda Weissmann, a prisoner in the camp. She was in the hospital for many months. Kurt visited Gerda almost every day and helped her get in touch with her only surviving relative, an uncle in Turkey. They fell in love. When he was sent to Munich in late June, he could no longer visit. He wrote letters to Gerda, who joined him in Munich at the end of July. Kurt was sent home to the United States in September 1945. He proposed to Gerda, but they had to wait to marry until her papers came through in 1946. Kurt ran a printing company in Buffalo, New York. It became clear that Kurt's parents and Gerda's family had not survived. Kurt and Gerda gave talks at various schools and other groups, and wrote books about their experiences, feeling it was their duty, as survivors, to do so.

Going into Hiding

People who did not get out of Germany early enough had to think of other ways to survive. One option was to go into hiding. Hiding was easiest for people who did not "look **Jewish**." **Nazi propaganda** showed Jews as having dark skin and heavy features. It was easier for blonde, blue-eyed Jews with fair skin to pretend to be **Aryans.**

Rosette Goldstein

This photo of Rosette Goldstein was taken during the war. Rosette, on the right, is with Mrs Martin, the farmer's wife, and her youngest daughter. The Martins took a risk in hiding Rosette and probably saved her life. But, despite their kindness, she never felt she fitted in. Many other hidden children felt the same.

Hidden Children

It was dangerous for a whole family to go into hiding. Many families split up—some only had the chance to hide one person, usually a child, who was hidden among non-Jewish people. These people took a big risk. Some children spent the entire war with one family. Others were moved around. Some of them were well looked after, while others were treated badly. All of them were scared by the separation. Many of them survived. They were often the only survivors from their families.

Rosette Goldstein

Rosette Goldstein's parents left Poland for France soon after Hitler came to power. Rosette was born in Paris in 1938. When the German army **occupied** France, the family was in danger again. In 1942 Rosette's father, who was working as a lumberjack, asked a local farmer to hide Rosette.

Into Hiding

The farmer agreed, so Rosette's mother put her on the train from Paris:

All of a sudden I was sent to this farm, to live with people I did not know. I remember going on the train with Jean Raffa, a friend of my father who was a Christian. I remember eating hard-boiled eggs and bread and butter and being warned that if anyone asked, I had to say he was my father. I was lucky, because my father was at the farm on the first night, so I felt safer.

There were good and bad aspects to life on the farm. Rosette remembers:

> We were lucky to always have food, because it was a farm. There were chickens. We made our own butter, even our own soap. There were three girls in the family. I can't say that I suffered, but I was lonely, I had no friends. They were good to me, but sometimes, if she was cross, the youngest, who was fourteen, would say things to me like "You dirty Jew." The girls were so much older than me, they were working on the farm all the time, they had no time for me, or if I got to do anything it was watch the cows all day with the youngest girl.

Nearly Caught

Rosette had to be careful not to be caught, but sometimes curiosity got the better of many of hidden children:

> One day I saw soldiers with rifles coming to the farm. They had come for food, for the chickens. The farmer's wife put me in the bedroom, under the mattress. I got out and went to look through the keyhole and I could see the Nazis standing in front of the chimney in the next room. I was lucky. They didn't search the place.

Reunited

Rosette's mother survived the war in Paris by pretending she was not Jewish. She was never caught. When the war ended, she went to find Rosette. They went back to Paris and began rebuilding their lives without Rosette's father, who had been killed at Auschwitz. Rosette found it hard to forget the war years, although she knows she was lucky:

> Nobody wanted to listen to us. They all said, "You were very lucky, that's it. Don't talk about it anymore." But I knew it made me different. When we hidden children meet, we are drawn together by the fact that we are different from other people. I didn't see myself as a **Holocaust** survivor at first. But that is what I am.

The Ghettos

As the **Nazis** took over Eastern Europe they set up **ghettos** and rounded up Jewish people into them. Ghettos were walled or fenced-off areas of a town or city where all Jews had to live. Once the ghettos were set up, Jewish people from Germany were sent there, and then Jews from **occupied** western Europe were crammed in as well. During the **Holocaust**, Jewish people were taken from the ghettos to the **camps.**

Zelda Polofsky

Zelda Polofsky was born in 1932, in a small town near Vilna in Lithuania, which was part of Poland before World War II. The Nazis occupied the village in 1941. Zelda remembers their arrival. The Jews from the village were rounded up into a town ghetto. Her father and some other men made a hiding place for several families, carefully dug under a building that had no basement, fearing that worse was to come.

A Narrow Escape

Zelda remembers they only just escaped the massacre in the Vilna ghetto. She had been ill and, waking early and feeling better, went for a walk:

> *It was only just light. I went down to the lake and saw a policeman with a gun there. He wasn't supposed to be there, so I went and told my mother, "Something doesn't feel right." So we*

Happier Times

This photo shows Zelda Polofsky, sitting down, and her older sister, Droysk, before the war. Droysk fell sick and died while in hiding.

> *went to the hiding place. As we went we could hear shooting, there were people running all over. People were running into the water of the lake, dragging their children. We hid for days. The men went out at night. They said all the houses were empty. They took what food they could find for us. The Germans had put out signs saying: "We know you are hiding. Don't be afraid. Come out and you will be safe, we will give you work." But we stayed put.*

They were found after five days in hiding, but were not shot at once. They were imprisoned but Zelda's father managed to bribe a guard to let ten men, women, and children leave the ghetto and go into hiding.

Hiding

A local farmer hid the runaways, but there were too many of them for him to hide for long. They moved to another farm but could not stay there long, either. There were so many of them, it was hard to stay hidden and people were soon talking about them. They went into hiding in the woods. The farmer brought them food when he could and they begged and stole food from other farmers. Zelda remembers:

> They begged from other farmers and at night, they took what they could from the fields—carrots, potatoes. I got sick and whatever food my family had was given to me. My mother gave me all the food; maybe it would have kept her alive. And I took it, never questioning.

A Death

Living in the woods in the rain and snow of winter, with hardly any food or shelter, was desperately hard. Sometimes some of them found shelter in a barn or shed, but seldom for long. The group eventually broke up. Then Zelda's mother became ill:

> We were hiding in a haybarn and my father had left to find food. My mother kept calling, calling for him. When he came at last she said, "You're here. Now I can die." And she did.

After the War

After the war, Zelda and her father spent some time in a **displaced person camp.** This card was given to Zelda when she left. It proved she did not have any infectious diseases.

Liberation

The family stayed in the woods for four years, until the end of the war. Zelda's sister died, but Zelda and her father survived, although they were both sick by the time they were **liberated** by the Russians. They went home and learned that only 27 of the 550 Jews that had lived in their town had survived. The remaining local people were hostile, blaming all Jews for the war. It was clear that they could not stay, so they moved on. They eventually settled in the U.S.

AJDC-CC-OSE MEDICAL DEPARTMENT

Health Card № 104534

(N)

Issued only to persons who were found free from disease or have been successfully treated.

Name: CYPUK ZELDA

Sex: F   15 XII. 35.

DICAL PURPOSES ONLY.

Signature

Fighting from Hiding

Many people who went into hiding had to concentrate solely on staying alive. On the other hand, some groups of people became **partisans.** They hid in the forests and fought the **Nazis** whenever they could. Depending on how they were armed and where they were hiding, they blew up roads, bridges, and railway lines, killed soldiers, stole supplies, and smuggled others to safety. Some groups were large and well organized. Some even had contact with the world outside Nazi Europe and were sent weapons, money, and other supplies.

Ruzka Korczak

Ruzka Korczak grew up in a **Jewish** community in Poland. She joined a **Zionist** youth group and was determined to go to live in Palestine. In 1939, when she was eighteen, Hitler invaded Poland. Ruzka made her way 300 miles (483 kilometers), mostly on foot, across Poland to Vilna, where she heard that Zionist youth groups were gathering to go to Palestine. She set up home there with some other Zionists, all about her age. Among these were two people who were to become her lifelong friends: Vitka Kempner and Abba Kovner.

In June 1940, the Russians took Vilna. The Zionist groups broke up. Some were arrested. The rest moved on. Ruzka headed for home, but the roads were blocked. She had to go back to Vilna, which had just been **occupied** by the Germans. She and Vitka were forced to live in the medieval Vilna **ghetto,** which had only six streets for 30,000 people. Because they had lived in Vilna for a while they were lucky—they knew someone who took them in. There were ten boys and two girls in just three rooms. Some Zionists joined the ghetto police. When two of them were on duty together at the gate they could smuggle food and weapons in and out. It soon became clear, though, that the Germans were moving more and more people out of the ghetto to an uncertain fate. Then news came that these people had been mass murdered in the nearby woods. It was time to act.

Fighting Together

This photo of Ruzka, Abba, and Vitka was taken in Vilna, shortly after the war ended.

16

Fighter and Caregiver

Ruzka, together with other partisans, fought the Nazis in the ghetto and later when they went into hiding in the woods. She was also in charge of their health and the very limited supply of food. When some bread was stolen, the thieves were caught and sentenced to death. Ruzka thought it was harsh, but right: "It was a powerful lesson. Stealing stopped in the camp."

The Partisans

Abba Kovner, the leader of the partisan group, held a ghetto meeting for the toughest young people his group could find. He explained that only 17,000 people remained of the 80,000 Jews that had once been in the ghetto. The rest had been murdered. He urged them to fight. Many agreed, and the partisans began to train them and to get weapons. Guns were smuggled into the ghetto from outside in many ways, including through the sewers by men posing as workmen laying pipes. The sewers were a good way to move around the city—inside and outside of the ghetto. Ruzka found a book, in Finnish, in the ghetto library. It described all sorts of methods of **guerrilla fighting**, including how to make cheap bombs. They began to follow the instructions. Ruzka also spent a lot of time walking the streets, trying to convince young people to join the resisters. Groups of partisans slipped out from the ghetto and blew up railway lines and caused other disruptions.

Living in Israel

This photo, taken in 1948, shows three survivors from Buchenwald farming fruit on a kibbutz, or shared farm, near Jerusalem.

They began leaving the ghetto in small groups, to set up a home in the forest. Once enough of them were out, the others, including Ruzka, tried to start a ghetto uprising. It failed because most people would not fight. The partisans left the ghetto and continued to fight from the Rudniki forest, about 12 miles (19 kilometers) away from Vilna.

They were there for two years. It was hard, especially as they had decided to stay a Jewish group, rather than join other partisan groups in the forest. The peasants would help other groups, but refused to help the Jews. Ruzka took part in many dangerous partisan actions, blowing up bridges, railways, and weapons trains. In 1944, the group destroyed 51 trains, hundreds of trucks, and dozens of bridges. After **liberation,** Ruzka finally got her wish and went to live in Palestine, as did Abba and Vitka.

Surviving the Camps

Beginning in 1938, **Jewish** people were sent to the **camps** for no other reason than being Jewish. It was not until 1941 that the **Nazis** set up **death camps** to do nothing but kill Jewish people as efficiently as possible. However, by that time, thousands of Jews had already died due to the horrific conditions in the camps, where they received the worst treatment of all the Nazis' prisoners.

Gerda Weissmann

Gerda Weissmann was born in Bielsko, Poland, on May 8, 1924. She was fifteen when the German army **occupied** Poland, in September 1939. Her father was ill when the German army marched in. The family had been warned of the danger. A telegram came from Gerda's uncle Leo in Turkey saying: "Poland's last hour has come. Dangerous for Jews to remain. **Visas** waiting for you in Warsaw embassy. Come at once."

Gerda's mother decided they had to wait until her father was better. The German occupation was completed with stunning speed. By September 4, the streets were full of soldiers and many local people were greeting them with cheers. Nazi **swastikas** appeared everywhere. That evening a neighbor called: "She told us that during the afternoon several Jews had been rounded up and locked in the synagogue, which was then set on fire. 'Men had better stay out of sight,' she whispered."

Trapped

It was dangerous to go out, dangerous even to answer the door: "We heard of German soldiers coming to a house for information and if a man answered the door they took him away; often that was the last the family saw of him." It was difficult to decide if it was safer to stay or to go. Some relatives who tried to escape had their train bombed, were rounded up by the army, and barely escaped being shot. They returned to hide with the Weissmanns. On October 17, letters came ordering all men between the ages of 16 and 50 to register to work for the Nazis. Gerda's brother Arthur and their cousin David went to register. The next day, Arthur left. He asked them not to go with him to the station. It was months before they heard from him again. Then they heard that he and David had escaped and were in hiding.

Before the war

This photo shows Gerda Weissmann at fifteen. It was taken in 1939, the same year that Germany invaded Poland.

Moving Around

This map shows Bielsko and the camps that Gerda worked in during the war.

Camps where Gerda was imprisoned

Changes in Bielsko

Bielsko was close enough to the German border to be pulled into Greater Germany. This meant that the Nazis were committed to making Bielsko *Judenfrei*—Jew free:

> *Late in November a letter came saying all Jews had to report on Monday, December 2, 1939, to a building in Hermann Goering Strasse. We had to leave our valuables and the keys for the house, clearly labeled, in the front hall of the house.*

The Weissmanns sold what they could but did not get much money for it. The next day, news came that the **deportation** had been postponed. Meanwhile, government actions against Jews became stricter:

> *After Christmas our rations were cut to less than half the rations of non-Jews. In the New Year we were ordered to wear white armbands with a blue star and the word JEW on them. Shortly after, this was changed to a yellow star.*

Many Jewish people left Bielsko, but the Weissmanns stayed. On April 19, 1942, the remaining 250 Jews in the town, mostly the old and the sick, were ordered to move to a small **ghetto**—just a few houses around a cobbled courtyard—set up in the poorest part of the town. In June the ghetto was broken up to make Bielsko *Judenfrei*.

Leaving Bielsko

The Weissmanns were told that Gerda's father was to go to one **labor camp,** and Gerda and her mother to another:

> *We were assembled in a field in Bielsko. After about four hours, the **SS** men finally came in a shiny black car, with their shiny boots. They checked lists. We were all there. Why did we all walk meek like sheep to the slaughterhouse? Why did we not fight back, run, hide? Because we did not think that human beings were able to commit the crimes that were being committed.*

They were divided up at the station. Gerda was put in a different group from her mother:

> *I knew Mama was marching on—in the other direction. I did not turn around. I knew that if I did so we would run to each other and they would beat us or shoot us. We had to go on alone.*

Gerda never saw her mother again. She was not entirely alone, though. A friend from Bielsko, Ilse, was with her.

Sosnowitz and Bolkenhain

Gerda's train took them to Sosnowitz **ghetto.** The girls were taken to a barracks until they were sent off as slave labor to a factory that asked the **SS** for workers. Gerda and Ilse were chosen to work in the Bolkenhain weaving mill and were taken there on July 2, 1942. The director of the factory made a speech: "We would be taught to weave. If we behaved and worked hard, all would be well; if not, we would be sent back."

The **Jewish** woman put in charge also made a speech:

> Frau Berger said, "How we feel is beside the point; we have to please the people here. I will personally punish anyone who breaks the rules. One person can make it hard for all of us." She had made it clear where we stood. She had also made it clear to the director that we were not fools. I liked her for that.

The barracks at Bolkenhain were new, so everything was fresh and clean. It was turning out to be one of the better **camps:**

> We were given warm soup in new bowls and hunks of good bread. After supper, we were allowed to wash, although the water was cold. After that, we were free to sleep.

Working at Bolkenhain

Gerda's day began at 5:30 A.M. and lasted until late in the evening. The girls were first taught to use the weaving looms and then moved on to work in the factory.

> We were very tense and frightened because we had been told that each mistake could be counted as an act of **sabotage.** We worked hard. At first we tended one loom, then two, then three, and finally four. It was exhausting. You had to run from loom to loom, eyes straining to follow the movement of the machine. The noise of the looms was deafening.

The girls did not have to work on Sundays and they were allowed to send and receive letters. These conditions were better than conditions in **concentration camps** or **death camps,** but they were still hard and the threat of being sent somewhere else was always there.

Moved On

In August 1943, the mill at Bolkenhain was closed. The war was going badly and there was not enough yarn for the machines. The girls were divided into groups. Gerda and Ilse managed to stay together and were taken to Marzdorf:

> *We were met by our new camp commander, a girl of about eighteen, tall and blonde. Whip in hand, she was shouting at the Jewish woman in charge of the workers. It was very different. My heart sank.*

Marzdorf was an older, more disorganized camp. The work was far harder, including stacking big bundles of flax, a straw-like fiber: "Our arms became bloody, swollen, and infected. The thick dust irritated eyes and wounds and made it hard to breathe."

As well as her mill job, Gerda had to work much of the night shoveling coal. Luckily, she and Ilse were among a group sent to Landeshut camp to work on weaving looms again. Here they only worked one shift, the night shift from 6 P.M. to 7 A.M. with a break in the middle for a bowl of soup. They were not allowed mail, but had Sundays off. Many of the girls were now friends and helped each other keep going. Even so, the work was hard and rations had been cut even more. Then, on May 6, 1944, the girls were told that they were going to a larger camp—Grunberg. The girls working in the spinning room at Grunberg regularly became ill and were sent to Auschwitz to be gassed.

Death march and Liberation

Gerda and her friends were put on the death march from Grunberg to Helmbrechts. There were 2,000 in Gerda's group. Only 120 lived through it. Gerda was one of them. Ilse was not.

By the time they were **liberated** Gerda says: "My mind was so dull, my nerves were so worn out with waiting, that I just sat and waited for whatever would happen next."

What happened next was that they were liberated by American soldiers. One of them was Kurt Klein (see pages 10–11), who visited Gerda in the hospital. They fell in love, married, and went to live in Buffalo, New York. They wrote several books about their **Holocaust** experiences and set up the Klein Foundation, which works to teach young people "tolerance for differences in others."

The Kleins Today

For many years, Gerda and Kurt gave talks about their wartime experiences. They felt that people needed to remember the Holocaust and learn tolerance for one another.

Political Prisoners

Jewish people suffered the worst treatment and conditions in the **camps.** However, there were other groups, too, that the **Nazis** saw as coming from inferior racial groups and who were also treated especially harshly. Two such groups were Russians and Poles, whom the Nazis saw as belonging to a **race** they labeled "Slavs."

Tadeusz Sobolewicz

Tadeusz Sobolewicz was only seventeen years old when he was arrested in 1941 as a "**political.**" He and his family had been involved in the Polish **resistance** movement, and he had been on the run for some time. He was imprisoned, questioned, and sent to Auschwitz I. Tadeusz remembers arriving in Auschwitz with a trainload of other politicals:

> The platform was full of **SS** guards. Each had a submachine gun or rifle. Some had dogs. Our guard opened the doors and undid the barbed wire [the prisoners had been bound together with this wire]. We tumbled out to shouted orders and suddenly, for no reason, the SS began hitting people. We were marched to the camp, where we were handed over to prisoners in striped uniforms, each armed with a pole or club, who marched us to "Reception."

At the "Reception" building the prisoners went through the usual processing:

> We were ordered to undress and put

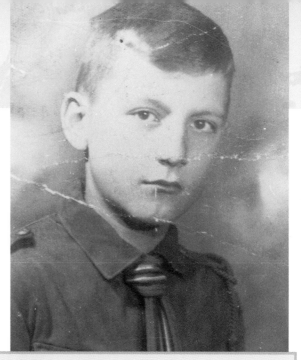

Happier Times

This photo shows Tadeusz Sobolewicz in his boy scout uniform. It was taken in 1935, when he was eleven years old.

> our belongings into paper bags. We handed these to **prisoner functionaries,** gave them our details, and were given a prisoner number. This number and our names were written on the bags, which they took away. Next, they shaved our heads. After that we had to walk, naked, to the bathhouse. I had not washed properly in months, so stepped eagerly into the shower. The water was almost boiling. "Too hot for you? I'll make it cooler," shouted the inmate at the controls. He made it freezing cold. We then had to line up, still naked, cold and dripping water, for underwear, uniforms, and wooden clogs. It took hours until I was finally handed the red triangular badge with my number, 23053. We were sorted into block groups and marched to those blocks. Standing outside, we were given needles and thread to sew our badges on. We had had nothing to eat all day.

Auschwitz

Tadeusz was in Block 9, with a few other people he knew from the resistance movement. Their block warden made them take off their shoes and crammed them into a bare room. They were each given a blanket but slept on the floor: "The five of us lay down together in the first space we could find. We were all cramped up like sardines in a tin."

A man, clearly unwell, who could not make it out of the room to the toilet in time, was beaten to death in the corridor. Tadeusz could not understand the continual shouting and brutality. One of the older men said: "Wise up, Tadio! They don't need a reason to beat us, they'll do it for nothing. Try not to put a foot wrong."

The prisoners were woken up early, with more shouting. They had to put their clothes on, hand in their blankets, and go to the washroom to splash water over their faces and hands:

> We had to line up in the corridor. At the end of the corridor, a **kapo** was ladling a sort of hot gray liquid into tins. Once this was drunk it was **roll call** in front of the block. We were lined up and taught what to do. It takes time to teach 400 prisoners how to take off their caps and put them back on at exactly the same time. Many newcomers did not speak German (orders were always given in German) and had no military training.

The Main Gates

This photo shows the main gates of Auschwitz I. The words over the gate say "Work will set you free" in German.

The rest of the block groups were sent to work. The prisoners from Block 9 were newcomers and had not yet been sorted into work groups. Block 9 had to work on following orders all together. They practiced roll call drill and also hopping like frogs. They were beaten over and over; several were beaten to death. Priests and Jews were hauled out of the line and either beaten to death or marched away for "special treatment." Then the group was marched off to be photographed, something that should have been done the day before, but the SS had run out of film.

Work

At about noon on the first day, Tadeusz and the other prisoners were given more "soup." They were then marched off to the yards by the station where the building materials were stored:

*Each of us had to take two bricks and return to the column, holding them level with our heads. We then had to run back to the main entrance, piling the bricks where the new blocks were being built. We then had to reassemble, run back, and go through the whole process again, but faster. If prisoners lost their grip on the bricks and dropped them this was **"sabotage"** and earned them a beating. We had to pass those who lay on the ground and keep going. Soon*

those of us left standing were out of breath, sweating, exhausted.

This process went on all afternoon. On the last return to the camp, the prisoners had to carry seven dead bodies, as well as the bricks. Work was followed by evening **roll call.** Next to the steps of the block lay the day's dead—they had to be counted, too. There were ten dead in all on the first day. After roll call, the prisoners were given a piece of bread and a spoonful of beetroot jam. Then it was bedtime:

Before we could collect our blankets and lie down, the block warden inspected our clothes, to make sure the triangles were properly sewn on. Again, there were several beatings. "We have to be so careful!" I thought. I was terrified and exhausted by the work, lack of food, and a whole day of trying not to get beaten up. I couldn't even cry.

Tadeusz's life in Auschwitz and the other **camps** he lived in later varied in many ways. He was given different work to do, all of it hard, some of it almost impossible. He was sometimes so ill he had to be taken to the hospital; he was always sick in some minor way because of the appalling living conditions. In one important way, every day he spent in the camps was the same as the first—the casual brutality, the beatings, and the fear were always there.

Exhausting Work

Prisoners in all of the camps had to do exhausting, often pointless, work all day. These prisoners are in Buchenwald camp.

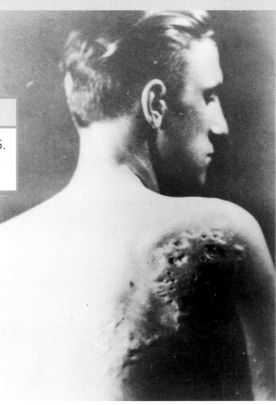

Liberation

Tadeusz was moved from Auschwitz to other camps: Buchenwald, Leipzig, Mulsen, Flossenbürg, and Regensburg. In April 1945, he and about 1,000 other Regensburg prisoners set off on a death march deeper into Germany:

> The **SS** surrounded the column; the march was very fast. After two hours, prisoners began falling behind. They were shot. I was at the front, pulling a food wagon. We managed to slow the column down, so that more people could keep up.

By the fourth day they had run out of food. There were far fewer prisoners—almost a third had died of exhaustion, been shot by the SS, or managed to slip away and hide. That night, several of the SS slipped away, too. The remaining SS kept the column marching and kept shooting the stragglers. By the fifth day, there were just 300 prisoners left. When they stopped at dawn, an SS officer came to the barn and said that Hitler was dead and that the SS officer in charge of the column had fled. In the morning, news came that the Americans were about 6.5 miles (10 kilometers) away. Tadeusz and his friends decided to hide in the barn and risk being found and shot on the spot. The villagers hid them until the American army arrived.

Going home

Tadeusz and his friends were told that they should report to a **DP (displaced persons) camp**:

> "Oh No!" No more camps, we decided. The American told us that we should at least go to one for long enough to have medical check-ups, but he would find us a place to stay outside the camp. He did. Next day, when I was examined, I was found to have TB. It was many months, in 1946, before I could go back to Poland.

When he got back, he found that his mother, who had been sent to Ravensbrück camp, had survived. His father had been gassed at Auschwitz. His younger brother had survived the war as part of a **partisan** group. When Auschwitz was set up as a museum, Tadeusz worked there, helping to make sure that the **Holocaust** was not forgotten. He still lives in Poland.

Hugo Gryn

Hugo Gryn was thirteen in April 1944, when the **Nazis** took over his hometown, Berehovo, in Czechoslovakia. Berehovo had been under Hungarian control since November 1938. The Hungarians were allies of the Nazis at this time. Thus, Hungarian was the official language and laws had been passed against **Jewish** people. Somehow people managed to carry on with their lives. The arrival of the Nazis increased the persecution at once. Soldiers marched in, took hostages, and demanded huge ransoms. The Nazis also set up **ghettos.** Hugo Gryn's memories here come from a statement he gave to officials in Budapest in July 1945, after he had returned home.

The Ghetto

Hugo remembers:

Part of Berehovo was cordoned off on April 20, 1944, and defined as a ghetto. Six thousand Jews came to the ghetto from the town alone, and as many from the surrounding areas. So the total number of Jews in the ghetto came to twelve thousand people.

Jewish people had been cut off from everyone else. The ghetto was very crowded. People were uprooted from their homes and crammed in with what few possessions they had been allowed to take.

The Journey

The ghetto was only intended to be a temporary stopping point. By this time, the Nazis had already decided on their "Final Solution" to what they called "the Jewish Problem." This solution was mass murder. Trains soon began running to what was, at first, an unknown destination—the **death camps.** Hugo's family were deported along with everyone else:

*On the 28th [of] May the **deportations** happened. I was put in a wagon along with the remaining Jews and my family—my parents and a younger brother. After a journey of three days, during which we suffered badly from thirst, we entered Auschwitz.*

Before the War

This photo, taken before the war, shows Hugo, his parents, and his younger brother, Gabi.

Berehovo's Children

Gabi's class in Berehovo's Jewish Elementary School, photographed in 1942–3. Every single child in this photo was gassed at Auschwitz.

Auschwitz-Birkenau

The three-day journey to Auschwitz in crowded wagons was exhausting. When they arrived at Auschwitz-Birkenau, Hugo and his family were herded off the train with everyone else, and their bags were taken. They then had to go through "selection," and this is when the family was broken up: "After arriving in Auschwitz we were divided up. I remained together with my father. My mother and my brother were snatched from us. . . ."

Hugo's brother, Gabi, was sent to the gas chambers of Auschwitz-Birkenau. The other prisoners told Hugo that this was the usual outcome for those not chosen to work. Hugo's mother was lucky not to be sent there, too. Shortly after their arrival at the camp, Hugo and his father heard that she had been sent to a women's **labor camp.**

Leaving Auschwitz

Those who were chosen to work at Auschwitz-Birkenau did not stay there long. There was no work in Auschwitz-Birkenau itself because it was a death camp. People there were simply waiting for their turn in the gas chambers. From time to time, a **transport** of workers was gathered together. Hugo's father decided that, no matter what skills were required, they should lie to get on to the next transport out. When the call came, it was for skilled building workers, and they stepped forward. They were chosen to go on the work transport. Hugo remembers: "Father and I remained only a week in Auschwitz, then we went in a work gang, which was intended for work in Lieberose, between Cottbus and Guben. The convoy consisted of 2,400 men, all Hungarian Jews."

Lieberose

Lieberose was a small camp, in the middle of the woods. It turned out to be one of the better **camps.** The workers there were being used to build a vacation town for German officers at Ullersdorf. They built the houses and drains and set up the electrical lines. While conditions here were better than in many camps, they were still bad, as Hugo recalls:

> *In Lieberose, we were used for building work, and barracks and houses made of stone were built. The work itself might have been okay because each person was employed according to their strengths. And we were housed in half-human quarters, so that we could sleep properly. But the treatment we had was unbearable. Punishments and other hard mistreatments were the order of the day, without us being even slightly at fault. As for the rest, we were worked almost to the death, with food so bad that we mostly left it.*

Marching West Through Germany

On February 2, 1945, Lieberose was evacuated ahead of the advancing Soviet army. Hugo and his father were well enough to take part in the death march, as they were healthier than many in the camp:

> *Now it was really clear what the health situation of the camp inmates was. Out of the 2,400 that came here [in Hugo's transport from Auschwitz], there were only 150 in a fit state to walk. The rest of them had to be left in the care of the hospital. After we left, the hospital was set on fire, and the people in the hospital all died.*

The prisoners (about 1,400 in all) had to walk to Sachsenhausen, which they reached on February 10. Five hundred of them died on the eight-day journey, which covered more than 100 miles (160 kilometers). They only stayed in Sachsenhausen for three weeks and then were marched on again, this time to Mauthausen.

Lieberose

Prisoners from Lieberose camp in Upper Silesia, Germany, pictured here, are connecting electricity to the site of the Ullersdorf vacation town.

Going Back

This photograph of Hugo Gryn was taken when he returned to Auschwitz in 1989.

This crowding meant that by morning, the weakest from the night before had been crushed to death. The camp was also full of contagious diseases. On May 4, 1945, the American 71st Division **liberated** Gunskirchen. The soldiers moved everybody to a clean German army barracks nearby, at Horsching. Hugo and his father had survived. Unfortunately, the death marches had badly weakened Hugo's father:

> *My father, who was then forty-five, had already found himself in a severely weakened condition by the time he came to Mauthausen because of the unbearable hardships, the marching, and the lack of food. Here he got very sick and died in the hospital on the 16th [of] May.*

Hugo spent six weeks at Horsching, recovering his strength and trying to come to terms with the death of his father, a death made worse by the fact that it happened so soon after their liberation. He was not yet fifteen years old. Hugo hoped that his mother would be alive, so he went back to Berehovo and she was there. While she was not yet ready to leave, she encouraged Hugo to leave Berehovo to carry on his education. He went to Prague, then Britain, and then moved to the United States to study to become a **rabbi**. Hugo married and had four children. He eventually settled in London and became famous as a broadcaster, as well as a rabbi. He died of cancer in 1996.

Mauthausen

By this time, most of the camps in the western part of German-controlled territory were in uproar because they were crammed with prisoners who had been marched from camps in the east. Some camps were shooting new arrivals on the spot, others put them in tents outside the camp, which were guarded by the soldiers who had marched them there. Mauthausen was, luckily for Hugo, one of these camps: "In Mauthausen we were kept in quarantine and stayed there for six weeks. Outside the **concentration camp**, a tented camp was set up, which housed the Hungarian workers."

Gunskirchen and Liberation

After six weeks, the Hungarian workers were marched off again, this time to Gunskirchen. They arrived there on April 16, 1946. Gunskirchen was very overcrowded, so much so that each night 2,500 prisoners were being shoved into huts that were supposed to hold 300.

Lucie Adelsberger

Lucie Adelsberger was living in Berlin and working as a doctor when the **Nazis** came to power. As a woman and a **Jew**, Lucie was someone the Nazis did not want working in the Nazi state. She was not allowed to work in the health service, and then she was not allowed to treat **Aryans** at all. Lucie's mother could not get a **visa** to leave Germany. Lucie remembers:

> *I loved my mother very much. When she fell sick I refused my last chance to emigrate. She had had a heart attack and needed care all the time. A nurse looked after her in the day and I cared for her at night. Should I let her be deported? I, as a doctor, could prevent it. I could save her by killing her, painlessly. I couldn't do it.*

Deportations

Deportations out of Berlin began. Lucie remembers:

> *How can anyone imagine what it's like to tremble at the arrival of the mail (three deliveries a day), expecting to be called to the **Gestapo,** or told by the **Judenrat** to evacuate on a certain date—you and your husband, or parents, or son, or anyone else you love. You learn to fear the doorbell, too, especially late at night.*

On May 6, 1943, she was arrested. On May 17 she was put on a **transport** to Auschwitz: "not from one of the main train stations, but from a small station on the outskirts of the north of Berlin, mostly surrounded by warehouses. The Gestapo liked to keep what it was doing quiet."

Wooden Barracks

These wooden huts, still standing in Auschwitz-Birkenau today, are the kind of huts the Gypsies were imprisoned in.

Arrival

The train arrived at Auschwitz-Birkenau two days later. Lucie remembers being marched to Auschwitz-Birkenau with about 260 other prisoners. They were stripped of all they had managed to hold onto in the unloading process, then shaved, showered, and given uniforms. Lucie and two other doctors were taken to the area of the camp where, for some reason, the Germans kept the **Gypsies** all together. All other groups were separated by age and sex. Various diseases had broken out in this part of the camp.

Working in the Hospital

The three doctors began work in the "hospital" at 4 A.M. the next morning. They joined a group of several so-called doctors and nurses, most of whom had no qualifications. Like all of the other barracks in this part of the camp, a wooden stable designed to hold 54 horses was now holding 800 to 1,000 people:

The doctors had hundreds of patients to care for. They had to fill out detailed notes for each of them every three days. They also had to keep a completely accurate count of their patients. There wasn't much time for treatment. There wasn't much medicine, either. The only thing we had in any quantity were sacks of a white powder called bolus alba. *We gave it as pills for stomach upsets, sprinkled it on wounds and rashes, and even mixed it up in a paste and painted the bunks and walls with it. All we could really do for the patients was to comfort and encourage them. It didn't make them any better; they still died like flies.*

On the night of July 31, 1944, the **SS** killed all of the Gypsies. Lucie was moved to the women's camp. On January 18, 1945, Lucie's part of the camp set off on a death march to Loslau, where they were crammed into open coal trucks and taken to Ravensbrück. There, the group was broken up and moved to smaller camps. They expected **liberation** at any time. The Americans finally reached the camp Lucie was in on May 2. Lucie went to live in the United States where she continued the work she had done before the war, researching allergies and infectious diseases. She died in 1971.

Surviving by Cooperating

Prisoners had a better chance of survival in the camps if they had an "easy" job. These jobs always had a cost. Sometimes a person was in charge of other prisoners and had to be brutal to them to keep the job. Other prisoners worked in the offices, keeping the **Nazi** system going. The worst job of all was clearing out the gas chambers in the **death camps.**

Fania Fénelon

Before the war Fania Fénelon, who was half **Jewish,** was a singer living in Paris. During the war, she continued singing and worked for the French **resistance.** She was arrested in 1943 and sent to Drancy camp. From there she was moved to Auschwitz-Birkenau on January 20, 1944. On the train she made friends with a woman named Clara, sharing her black market food with her.

Fania remembers arriving at Auschwitz:

*We had been traveling for over fifty hours. The smell was dreadful. At first, supervised by the **SS,** the men in each carriage had emptied the toilet buckets, but that didn't last. Our bucket had emptied itself by overturning. We were desperately thirsty. The air was stinking and no fresh air was coming in. We were suffocating. Our door was opened; everyone rushed to it. We were told to get out, to leave the luggage. SS soldiers climbed in and threw out the ill, the slow, and the corpses. Living skeletons in striped uniforms, their skulls shaven, moved among us, took the luggage, carried it away. Trucks drove up, with red crosses in white circles on them. "The Red Cross is here," said Clara. "We're not in any danger."*

Chosen to Live

Fania and Clara were not loaded onto the trucks, which were not actually Red Cross trucks, but trucks that took people to the gas chambers of Birkenau to be killed. Fifty men and fifty women were chosen to live from that **transport** of about 1,200. They were marched through the snow for half an hour until they arrived at Auschwitz-Birkenau: "We were herded towards a brick building marked 'Reception Block.'"

Drancy

Fania spent nine months in Drancy camp in France before she was sent to Auschwitz-Birkenau.

Uniforms

This photo shows some uniforms now on display at Auschwitz. By January 1944, there were so many prisoners that the camp was running out of uniforms. Clothes stored from earlier arrivals were used, often with a broad blue stripe painted on them, until enough people died for there to be spare uniforms again.

A Vital Conversation

Fania had only been in Auschwitz for a day before she had an unexpected opportunity of a better chance of survival:

In the middle of the babel [confusion] *a Polish woman was shrieking for* Madam Butterfly. *"What's she saying?" I asked.*

"She's looking for musicians, for the orchestra." An orchestra here? I must have misunderstood.

"What did you say?" I insisted.

"The orchestra, let it drop. What does it matter to you?"

"But I can play the piano and sing Madame Butterfly."

"Well, go and tell her."

I leaned over, tried to attract her attention. She didn't see me. I was forbidden to get down, but I did. In a fog, aching all over, I hobbled over to the huge **kapo.** *She stared at me suspiciously. I was so small, so dirty, spattered with mud and blood.*

"Follow me."

First Days at Auschwitz

At the "Reception Block," Polish girls filled out forms about the prisoners. Prisoners were stripped and then shaved. Fania remembers: "Tattooing came next. I watched as the number 744826 appeared on my forearm. By now I had understood. I was no longer anything, not even a slave."

They were kept waiting in a large building for some hours and then ordered out:

My bare feet were awkward in the men's shoes I had been given, one yellow shoe and one black boot, about size ten, when I took a size four. How could I march in line or keep in step with these on my feet?

Fania and the others were taken to one of the brick barrack blocks. Fania asked the block warden what had happened to the people in the trucks. She did not reply at first. Then Fania was dragged to the door: "She pointed to a smoking chimney: 'You see that smoke, over there? That's your friends, cooking.' 'All of them?' 'All of them.'"

Chosen for the Orchestra

Fania was taken to a large, warm, well-lit room. She was told to play the piano and sing. She was told she could join the orchestra. Taking a huge risk, she demanded that they take Clara, too. They did, because Clara could sing beautifully. Clara and Fania were given clothes that fit. Fania was even given a pair of fur-lined boots. Their barracks was clean and they each had a bed with a sheet and a blanket. They were allowed to shower every day. But, they were not safe. As Fania was told when she arrived: "We were set up on a whim and we could vanish on one, too."

Pleasing the SS

The girls who had been in the orchestra for a while told Fania that the **SS** wanted to hear famous music, even though there were not enough girls to play and some of them did not play very well.

Fania took on the job of rewriting the music the SS wanted to hear so that the girls could play it:

> *We did seventeen hours of music a day. Then there were the concerts for the SS, whenever they called for them, to relax after their "hard" work. It was pleasing the SS at these concerts that kept us alive.*

The orchestra had to keep playing, to do their best, even in the most awful circumstances. At one concert, Fania remembers:

> *I saw one woman run up to the electric fence and grip the metal. Her body twisted violently, shaken by the current. A friend rushed forward to pull her off and was also fixed to the wire by the current. No one moved. The music played on; the SS listened and talked among themselves.*

Camp Orchestra

This photo shows the men's orchestra at Auschwitz I. Several other camps also had orchestras.

Last Days

As the **Allies** advanced, rumors floated around Auschwitz that the **Nazis** were losing. Fania noticed: "Our SS seemed uneasy, their morale was crumbling."

But they did not slow down the killing. Instead, they worked faster, running the **crematoria** day and night—24,000 bodies a day. The orchestra was broken up. Fania and some others were marched to Bergen-Belsen, which was full. They were put into leaky tents nearby. Fania caught typhus and nearly died, as did many of the others. The SS were told to burn and destroy the camp on April 15, 1945: "We were to be shot at 3 P.M. The British arrived at 11 A.M."

Liberation

When the British arrived, Fania was very ill, but knowing they had been **liberated** gave her hope. Her friends asked her to sing. She did so:

I straightened up and sang the Marseillaise *(the French national anthem). A Belgian officer handed me the most wonderful present: an old lipstick. I couldn't think of anything lovelier, despite it being three-quarters used by a total stranger. The person with the microphone said: "Please, Miss, it's for the BBC." I sang* God Save the King *(the British national anthem), then the* Internationale *(the Russian national anthem). The Russian prisoners joined in. I sang and from all the corners of the camp dying skeletons stirred, got up, grew taller. A great "Hurrah" burst out—they had become men and women again.*

Remembering

Fania survived and so did some other members of the orchestra. In her book about her experiences, *Playing For Time*, she says: "I think I've achieved more or less what I wanted for myself now. I wanted to sing, and I've done that now for 25 years."

However, she has not forgotten Auschwitz: "Particularly at night I find myself back in the block at Birkenau. I spend every night there—every night! I've never left the camp, not for thirty years."

Elie Cohen

Elie Cohen was a doctor in Aduard, a village near Groningen in the Netherlands, when war broke out in 1939. He was 30 years old. In May 1940, the German army took over the Netherlands. On February 8, 1941, Elie and his wife and baby son moved to Groningen and lived there in hiding. They planned to escape to Sweden, but were caught by the **Gestapo** and arrested.

Separated

A relative persuaded the Gestapo to give him the Cohen's two-year-old baby. Elie's wife was put in prison. Elie was sent to Amersfoort **labor camp.** Luckily, a nurse in the women's camp knew him: "She got me a job looking after American prisoners in a nearby camp. I was given more food. I was not beaten anymore and this saved me."

On December 8, 1942, Elie was moved to Westerbork camp. The **SS** decided to keep him on as a doctor, rather than send him straight to the **camps** in the east.

Collaborating

Elie's wife was allowed to join him at Westerbork: "We shared a small flat with a German **Jewish** couple. I had a red stamp on my identity card that said I was not to be transported to Auschwitz."

Elie bought his safety at a price:

> *I became the transport doctor. I had to examine Jews selected for **transports** to the east. I could say a person was unfit for transport. If I did this, he and his family were spared. I faked high temperatures and so on to save people.*

Dr. Spanier, the senior camp doctor, found out what Elie was doing and warned him that if he continued, it would be his family that was transported:

> *So I knuckled under. I collaborated. It is a terrible word, but I cannot escape it although my situation was impossible. We did the Germans' jobs for them. I don't know if I would have done it if I had known what would happen to them. We were told they were going to work camps.*

Westerbork Transport

These people leaving Westerbork camp have been passed as fit to travel by a camp doctor.

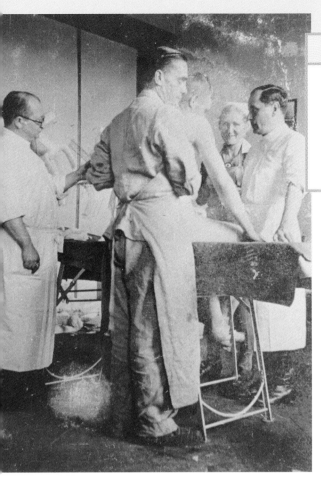

The Wrong Choice

On April 9, 1943, the **Nazis** began to hunt harder outside the camps for Jews. Elie decided their son would be safer in Westerbork, protected by Elie's job. Shortly after this, his wife was accused of saying anti-German things and their protected status was taken away. Two weeks later the family was sent to Auschwitz:

The selection was made as soon as we arrived. We didn't know what it meant. I waved goodbye to my wife, son, and mother-in-law. A couple of hours later a Dutch Jew came up and congratulated me. I asked him why. "Because you are in a work camp and the others are dead," he said. The strange thing is I believed it

at once—I accepted it. And I wanted to survive.

Elie managed to get work as a doctor in the medical blocks at Auschwitz.

Collaborating Again

Elie found he had to do awful things to keep his job, to survive:

I had to help the SS doctor, Klein, in his selections. He chose those among the Jewish patients who he thought were no longer worth treating. I had to produce their medical cards and tell him my opinion of their condition. It was useless to pretend, because he could see the state they were in, but we played out the little scene, over and over. And I took part, because I wanted to live.

After the War

Elie made his way back to the Netherlands, where he settled in Arnhem. He married again and had two children. He wrote a book called *Human Behavior in the Concentration Camp* and worked as a psychiatrist, specializing in helping survivors to deal with their feelings.

Surviving by Escaping

There were people who were swept up in the **Holocaust** but managed to escape. Men, women, and children escaped from **ghettos,** from **transports,** even from **camps.** Depending on their age, sex, and appearance, they hid in different ways. Some spent all of their time hiding. Others managed to join **partisan** or **resistance** groups and fought back.

Ruth Cyrus

Ruth Cyrus was 29 when Germany invaded Poland. She and her husband, George, were both **Jewish** and both lawyers. Ruth was pregnant. As soon as the Germans invaded, George was called into the Polish army and Ruth did not see him again until the end of the war. Once the Germans took Warsaw, Ruth could no longer work as a lawyer. Her daughter, Eva, was born on March 4, 1940.

In the Ghetto

In October the Warsaw ghetto was set up, surrounded by high brick walls with splinters of glass and barbed wire on top. In July 1942, the Germans began to transport large numbers of Jews out of the ghetto for **"resettlement."** A couple of months later, a young man appeared and told us the resettlement trains were going to Treblinka, where people were gassed to death. He had managed to escape hidden under piles of clothes being taken back to the ghetto. Ruth made a decision: "I would not let myself be taken to Treblinka. I would not let them gas me. When they caught me I would make my escape."

Ruth managed to get a thin hacksaw blade and practiced with the blade for hours on end: "From the moment I had the blade and had learned to make use of it, I felt somehow quieter and I knew they would not get me alive to Treblinka."

The German Invasion

This photo shows German troops occupying Warsaw in October 1939. The Germans completed their occupation of Poland with blistering speed.

Transported

Ruth and Eva managed not to be selected during several German round-ups. Partly this was because Ruth worked for a large factory in the ghetto, but it was also due to luck and quick thinking. Their turn came eventually. They were taken down to the station and shoved into cattle cars. Ruth saw that their cattle car had a high, barred window. Ruth asked two young men to hold her up to saw through the bars. Sawing through bars in a moving train was very difficult: "My fingers started bleeding, my hand became weak but I kept on sawing." The blood dripping from Ruth's fingers made the bars slippery and harder to saw.

The Jump

At last, after several hours, the job was done. Ruth knew she could not throw Eva out of the window—she would resist. Ruth decided she would have to go first, so someone had to throw Eva. Ruth promised all her food to anyone who would help. Two boys agreed:

"I'd like to jump first," said one of the boys who had lent me his shoulders. He put his hands against the window frame and jumped. The wind swept him off and that was all.

Before the War

This photograph of Ruth Cyrus was taken in Warsaw before the German invasion.

Now it was Ruth's turn. She had to ignore Eva's screams:

"Mommy, mommy, please don't jump." I plugged my ears. For a moment I concentrated on the technique of the jump itself and, standing on the second boy's shoulders, I grabbed the frame and thrust myself out legs first. I heard the whistle of the wind as I was whirled away. I lost consciousness.

What Happened Next?

Ruth woke to find she had been robbed, but the robbers had left her coat, her boots, and her hacksaw blade. After a frantic search, she found Eva. They were still in Poland. She spent the rest of the war as a "submarine," pretending she was not Jewish. She found someone to take Eva into their family. After the war, she and Eva and George finally got in touch using the various organizations set up to reunite families. They moved to South Africa.

Escape from a Camp

The **Nazi camps** were heavily guarded, day and night, to prevent escape. Despite the guards, people did escape, although many were caught again. The people who had the best chance of staying free were those who made contact with local **resistance** groups, or those who spoke the same language as the local people and could ask for help in a familiar language.

Vrba and Wetzler

Rudolf Vrba and Alfred Wetzler escaped from Auschwitz-Birkenau camp in April 1944. They had been brought to the camp in 1942, from Slovakia. Rudolf, aged seventeen, first worked sorting the luggage of the arrivals at Auschwitz-Birkenau. He was amazed by "Canada," the huge complex of sheds where possessions were sorted and stored:

> It was an incredible sight, a huge rectangular yard, fenced and guarded. There were several huge storerooms and mountains of trunks, cases, rucksacks, and kitbags. I didn't think then where their owners might be—every step brought some new shock.

Rudolf later worked as a clerk, registering new arrivals. When Rudolf found out that the killings were going to increase, he decided to escape.

He wanted to tell the world what was going on: "The **SS** were talking about 'Hungarian salami' and 'a million units'; it was clear what was going to happen."

Rudolf hoped the outside world would force the Nazis to stop the killing: "Panic and active resistance by a million people would have caused havoc in Hungary. That would be better than panic by the burning pits of Birkenau."

He and a friend, Alfred Wetzler, planned their escape carefully. The SS were extending the camp, and work parties were moving building materials around and digging trenches and pits in an area called "Mexico." Rudolf and Alfred decided to sneak into "Mexico" and make themselves a hiding place in a trench just deep enough for two, covered in a heap of wooden planks stored for use. They hid ordinary clothes, some food, water, and money in the trench.

MINISTERSTVO NÁRODNEJ OBRANY

Čj. 15550/34/Vr-50

Kleg. 5. oddel. 1946

Vlastnoručný podpis majiteľa

Rudolf Vrba

This photo shows Rudolf Vrba's 1946 Czechoslovakian identity card.

The Auschwitz Report

The Auschwitz report, and several documents summarizing it, were translated and sent to all of the Allied leaders.

Free!

On April 7, 1944, Rudolf and Alfred slipped into "Mexico" and hid in their trench. They were helped by friends in the camp resistance who piled wood over them and then sprinkled gasoline and tobacco around the pile. These strong smells kept the search dogs from smelling the hidden prisoners. They knew they would be missed at **roll call** and that there would be guards and dogs out searching for them. So, they did not try to get away at once. They stayed in the trench for three days. Finally, they climbed out at night and made their way south, away from Auschwitz. They had memorized lists of where people had come from, their numbers, and names. With the help of local people along the way, they made it to Slovakia, mostly on foot. They got in touch with a **Jewish** doctor who had not been deported because the SS desperately needed doctors:

> *I walked into Dr. Pollack's surgery, pretending to be a patient. I explained who I was and where I was from. When he heard that all his "resettled" relatives were dead, he became very shaky. He asked how he could help. I told him we had to get in touch with the Jewish Council in Bratislava.*

Dr. Pollack put Rudolf and Alfred in touch with the Jewish Council in Zilina. They

EXECUTIVE OFFICE OF THE PRESIDENT
★WAR REFUGEE BOARD
WASHINGTON, D.C.

4

GERMAN EXTERMINATION CAMPS — AUSCHWITZ AND BIRKENAU

It is a fact beyond denial that the Germans have deliberately and systematically murdered millions of innocent civilians — Jews and Christians alike — all over Europe. This campaign of terror and brutality, which is unprecedented in all history and which even now continues unabated, is part of the German plan to subjugate the free peoples of the world.

So revolting and diabolical are the German atrocities that the minds of civilized people find it difficult to believe that they have actually taken place. But the governments of the United States and of other countries have evidence which clearly substantiates the facts.

The War Refugee Board is engaged in a desperate effort to save as many as possible of Hitler's intended victims. To facilitate its work the Board has representatives in key spots in Europe. These representatives have tested contacts throughout Europe and keep the Board fully advised concerning the German campaign of extermination and torture.

Recently the Board received from a representative close to the scene two eye-witness accounts of events which occurred in notorious extermination camps established by the Germans. The first report is based upon the experiences of two young Slovakian Jews who escaped in April, 1944 after spending two years in the Nazi concentration camps at Auschwitz and Birkenau in southwestern Poland. The second report is made by a non-Jewish Polish major, the only survivor of one group imprisoned at Auschwitz.

wrote a long report about Auschwitz-Birkenau. Shortly after this, two more Auschwitz escapees arrived in Zilina. They confirmed Rudolf and Alfred's report and said the murder of Hungarian Jews had begun. The Jewish Council combined these two reports and smuggled it out of German-controlled Slovakia to Switzerland. From here it was sent to London and Washington, D.C. The American and British governments were slow to act, but they did eventually put pressure on the Hungarian government to stop the **deportation** of Jews. Rudolf and Alfred joined the Slovakian **partisans** and fought for the rest of the war. Rudolf went to Israel after the war, and then moved to Britain. He finally settled in Canada, working at the University of Vancouver. Alfred stayed in Bratislava, working as a newspaper editor.

Different Chances

Jewish people in different parts of Europe had very different chances of survival. People in Denmark worked hard to protect the Jews living there—and many of them escaped the **Nazis.** On the other hand, people in the east, especially those in the path of the ***Einsatzgruppen,*** were much less likely to survive the Nazi takeover. The *Einsatzgruppen* marched into towns and villages, rounded up all of the Jewish people, made some of them dig a huge pit nearby, and then shot them all. People were also affected by luck—good and bad. The mostly Jewish town of Eishyshok in Lithuania was massacred by the German army. A small number of people were lucky enough to get away. On the other hand, Leon Greenman, an Englishman living in the Netherlands, and his family had appallingly bad luck.

The Jews of Eishyshok
Eishyshok was a shtetl—a market town where most people were Jewish. As the German army marched east, Lithuania was in a direct line between Germany and the Soviet Union. On June 23, 1941, the German army reached Eishyshok. The **Gestapo** moved in, bringing with them an increasing number of anti-Jewish laws and ever more ways to humiliate people.

On September 21, the leader of *Einsatzkommando 3* arrived with a large number of armed Lithuanians. Some people began to slip away. Others stayed. Families split up, hoping that at least some would survive. The people of Eishyshok were locked up in the old synagogue for three days without food, water, or the use of a toilet. They were then taken to the Horse Market, a large open space where horses were sold. The *Einsatzkommando 3* lists say that on September 27, 1941, they killed 3,446 Jews—989 men, 1,636 women, and 821 children. In fact, by September 27, all of the Jews of Eishyshok were gone. About 5,000 were killed by *Einsatzkommando 3*. The men were killed on September 25, the women and children on September 26. They were killed in the Old Cemetery, where deep trenches had been dug to keep the cattle out. The trenches became ready-made graves.

Einsatzgruppen Shooting

This photo shows an *Einsatzgruppen* shooting in September 1941 in Dubossary in present-day Moldova. The soldiers killed 2,000 Jews that day.

Partisans

Many of those who escaped the *Einsatzgruppen* murders joined partisan groups in the forests, just as Zvi Michaelowski did. They fought the Nazis from their hiding places. These partisans fought in the Rudnika forest, near Eishyshok. Zvi fought with a group of partisans in the same forest for a while.

In Hiding

The Jews who escaped from Eishyshok fled to the nearby forests. During the war, the forests of Eastern Europe were full of groups of people, many of them Jewish, but also Poles and Russians. Some hid in small groups of three or four; some set up family camps. Others set up **partisan** groups to fight the Germans. Zvi fought with the partisans during the war. He was one of just 114 Jewish people from Eishyshok to survive the massacre and the war years by hiding in the forest.

After the war, Zvi was arrested by the Russians. He was sentenced to six years in Siberia, but he managed to escape on his way there. He found friends who gave him false **papers** and he made his way into Poland. Zvi ended up in a **(DP) displaced persons** camp called Bad Reichenhall, near Munich. He got married there, and he and his wife tried to get to Palestine. The first ship they went on, the *Exodus*, was forced to turn back, but they finally made it in 1947.

Zvi Michaelowski

Zvi Michaelowski was sixteen when the Germans invaded Lithuania. He escaped from Eishyshok with his sister when the *Einsatzgruppen* arrived. When he came back for more of his family, he was caught. He was in one of the last groups of men taken to the Old Cemetery on September 25. When they arrived they saw the trenches full of dead people. They were lined up along the edge of the trench. Just before the squad began to shoot, Zvi's father shoved him into the grave. Zvi was soon covered in bodies.

He lay there for a long time: "It got darker and darker. It was wet, hot and stifling. There were the sounds of those not quite dead moaning and the odd shot. Then it went quiet." Zvi pushed his way out of the heaps of bodies and crawled out of the grave.

Leon Greenman

Leon Greenman was born in London in 1910. In 1935, he married Else Van Dam and they moved to Rotterdam in the Netherlands to care for Else's grandmother. By the time their son Barney was born, on March 17, 1940, war had broken out. Both Leon and Else were British citizens, so Barney was British, too. While registering Barney's birth at the British embassy, Leon arranged to leave for Britain with the embassy workers. But events moved too fast. On May 14, the German army began to bomb Rotterdam. The bombing totally destroyed the center of the city, killing almost 1,000 people and leaving about 78,000 people homeless. The embassy people moved out at once, and the Greenman family was stranded.

Nazi rule

The **Nazis** took over the Netherlands with great speed and began passing laws against **Jewish** people. Leon, who was Jewish, could no longer trade with non-Jews. Making money was not the only problem. Leon remembers: "Our circle of friends was getting smaller and smaller. Every day we heard of people being taken out of their homes and never being seen again."

Leon accepted the offer of the Van Nautas, non-Jewish friends of friends, to look after the Greenmans' valuables. He gave them the family savings, his most valuable books and pictures, and their British passports: "I did not trust the Nazis. I thought that, if I were arrested, they would take the passports away and we would have no proof of our British nationality."

When Leon went back to collect the passports, he found that the Van Nautas had burned them because they were afraid the Nazis would find out they were helping Jews. So, the Greenman family had no passports. The British embassy people had left, so the Swiss were dealing with all British citizens. Leon wrote and visited the Swiss embassy over and over, begging for **papers** to prove the family was British. The papers had not yet come when the Greenmans were arrested in the middle of the night and sent to Westerbork camp.

Leon, Else, and Barney

This photo of Leon, Else, and Barney was taken in 1942, just a few months before they were arrested by the Nazis.

A Hopeful Message

Leon Greenman sent this telegram to his sister Kitty in England from a hospital in Paris. At this point, he was still hoping that Else and Barney were still alive.

Westerbork

In October 1942, the Greenman family arrived at the nearest station to Westerbork camp in the pouring rain:

> We had to walk the three miles there. It was muddy and walking was difficult. Else carried Barney and a bundle. I carried several bundles, with blankets draped around me. They fell off into the mud over and over.

At Westerbork the family was separated. Leon asked the chief administrator, Kurt Schlesinger, to put them in the care of the Red Cross as British citizens. They waited, visiting the office each day, increasingly worried because: "Once or twice a week, to make room for the new arrivals, about 1,000 Jews were sent to Auschwitz."

People did not know what went on in Auschwitz, but they did not want to go. One of Leon's friends in Westerbork, Michael Borstrock, escaped **deportation** by complaining of severe stomach pains. He was operated on for an ulcer. When the wound was almost healed he was called again: "Michael tore open his stomach wound to go to [the] hospital again."

Auschwitz and After

In mid-January 1943, the Greenman family was deported to Auschwitz. Leon later heard that a letter saying the family was British and should not be deported arrived the same morning their train left. "We had been told we were being sent to Poland to work for the Germans. We thought we might be separated but be able to see each other at weekends."

They were separated on the platform of Auschwitz-Birkenau. Leon saw Else and Barney loaded into a truck: "Else had made two red velvet capes for herself and Barney from curtains, and I could see the hoods. I did not know it was the last I would ever see of them."

It was. Else and Barney were driven off to the gas chambers. Leon had been selected for work. He survived life in Auschwitz, where he spent much of his time working in the Monowitz factory. He also survived a death march from Auschwitz to Buchenwald where he was **liberated** by the Americans on April 11, 1945. He discovered that only two people from his **transport** to Auschwitz—he and Michael Borstrock's brother, Leon—had survived. He returned to the Netherlands to find his father was still alive, but he decided to settle in England, where he lives now.

Feelings About Survival

We have seen that survivors of the **Holocaust** had very different experiences. However, all survivors shared one experience. They survived. They had spent their time in hiding or in the **camps** or fighting the **Nazis,** waiting and hoping to survive. Many were too ill, at first, to realize that the war was over, that they had survived. Eventually that fact became clear to the survivors. Their feelings about survival varied.

Feeling Angry

One would expect the survivors to feel angry with the Nazis, with the local people who had not helped them, with anyone and everyone they could blame for what had happened to them.

In fact, many survivors did not feel angry at all.

Elie Wiesel, who wrote about his camp experiences in a book called *Night*, remembers:

> *Our first act as free men was to throw ourselves on the food. We thought only of that. Not of revenge, not of our families. Nothing but bread. And even when we were no longer hungry, there was still no thought of revenge.*

Harry Spiro, just seventeen when the war ended, remembers being **liberated** in Terezín: "The Russian soldiers gave us 24 hours to do whatever we wanted, even kill the Germans. I don't think any of us did that, I'm not sure why."

A few days after he had been liberated, Jack Rubinfeld, just sixteen, was searching for food near the **labor camp** where he had been a prisoner. He found two loaves of bread:

> *A German woman with two small children asked for food, saying they had not eaten for a day. I looked around, ashamed to let my friends see. I broke off half a loaf and gave it to them.*

Free at Last

This photo shows prisoners in Buchenwald in the days after liberation. Elie Wiesel is in the second row of sleeping shelves from the bottom, second section from the left, by the far post.

How the Helpers Felt

Some of those who had helped many people survive as part of an escape route were, quite simply, relieved. One escape route member, interviewed in the 1980s, said:

> *I wept with joy. At last I could put down the heavy weight I had been carrying for years. I had needed to help, but I knew it put me in great danger. So, I'm sorry to say that my first reaction was as much happiness for myself as for all those Jewish people who were now safe.*

Other people, like Irene Gut Opdyke, had helped fewer people, but these people

had become friends. She found them in Kraków after the war: "I felt like a mother hen who finally has her chicks together again."

Oskar Schindler also kept in touch with "his" Jews after the war. The photo shows Schindler in the 1950s with some of the people he saved.

Feeling Lost

Many survivors had spent years in the camps, being told they were worthless, being treated appallingly, being told what to do every minute of every day. Harry Green remembers:

> *It took a long time to get used to being individuals again. I began to discover that I was a person in my own right—quite a revelation after years of **propaganda** about "vermin" and "parasites."*

Primo Levi, an Italian **Jew** who later wrote extensively about the Holocaust, remembers the first day of freedom:

> *For the whole day we had been too busy to remark on the event which we still felt marked the crucial point of our entire existence. Perhaps, unconsciously, we had looked for things to do to avoid spare time because, face to face with liberty, we felt ourselves lost, emptied, frozen, unable to play our part.*

Having forced himself to survive, having forced himself to stay fit, Levi now fell sick: "It seemed as if weariness and illness, like ferocious and cowardly beasts, had waited in ambush for the moment when I dismantled my defenses, in order to attack me from behind."

Talking it Through

Some survivors wanted to talk about their experiences, like this survivor photographed with an American soldier after liberation. The photo was posed, but there were many cases of soldiers who became friends with the people they liberated. They visited and listened and often tried to help people figure out what to do once they left the hospital.

Feeling Alone

Many survivors had longed to go home, but not all rushed off when they were **liberated.** Fania Fénelon remembers:

Waiting to be repatriated [returned to her country], *which naturally required paperwork, we stayed in the* **camp.** *It didn't worry us. Oddly enough, we were no longer in such a rush to get back. Normal life worried us; we no longer had the words or the gestures for it. Worse still, who would be waiting for us at the station? Were those for whom we had kept ourselves alive still living? We were still ill, still weak. Life worried us, because we were afraid.*

Edith Kramer-Freund was a German **Jew** whose husband had died before the war and who spent the war in Terezín. She was sent to Switzerland as part of a group rescued by the Red Cross before the end of the war. She remembers the shock that she and her fellow passengers got when they reached freedom:

It was a shock to find that we would not, from now on, get preferential treatment. We had held on until liberation. Now we had to fend for ourselves in war-time conditions.

Feeling Threatened

Many survivors who wanted to go home found that they could not. The **Nazi Holocaust** had been stopped, but there were still Polish and Russian **anti-semitic** groups hunting down and killing Jews. Harry Balsam, Chaim Ajzen, Ben Helfgott, and Roman Halter were all boys about sixteen years old who had been liberated from Terezín. They all tried to make their way home, to various parts of Poland. All turned back because of threats or stories of Polish groups killing any Jews they could find. They found it incredible that this could be happening after the Holocaust. They joined a group of children nicknamed "the Boys" who went to live in England. Eastern Europe no longer felt safe.

Coping with Freedom

When the **Allies** liberated the camps, they found many survivors in need of urgent medical attention. Survivors who were not sick, like these from Ebensee Camp, had to look after themselves as best they could.

Feeling Guilty

Many survivors felt guilty that they survived when so many millions did not. This feeling was worst among people who had collaborated to survive, such as Elie Cohen (see pages 36–37). But even Jews who left Germany before Hitler came to power, like Frederick Kramer who went to live in Australia in 1932, say they feel guilty because they think: "if my life had taken a slightly different turn, it could have been me, I could have ended up in the camps, I could have died. Why have *I* survived when so many died?"

Simon Wiesenthal was a prisoner in the camps. After the war he helped people find their relatives and then became famous for his work in tracking down Nazis. He thinks that all survivors feel guilt:

> *No matter how hard you try, no matter how hard you bury the camp experience under a successful later life, that feeling grips you, even if you know that you did not harm anyone else in order to survive.*

Needing to Remember

Many survivors talk to schoolchildren and students. Some conduct tours of the camps they were imprisoned in. They do this because they feel strongly that young people must be taught about the camps, must be told about those who did not survive by those who did, those who were there, whose experiences cannot be denied. Primo Levi explains:

> *For the survivors, remembering is a duty. They do not want to forget and, above all, they do not want the world to forget. They understand that their experiences were not meaningless, that the camps were not an accident, an unforeseeable historical happening. In every part of the world, wherever you begin by denying basic liberties, by denying equality, you move toward the camp system and it is a road on which it is difficult to halt.*

Timeline

1933

January 30	The **Nazi** Party comes to power in Germany. Adolf Hitler, its leader, is elected Chancellor.
February 27	Fire breaks out at the Reichstag, the German Parliament.
February 28	German President Hindenburg's decree "For the Protection of the People and the State" allows for the creation of **concentration camps.** The Nazis persuaded Hindenburg to pass the decree to fight what they called the "Communist threat" afte the fire at the Reichstag.
March 17	The **SS** is set up, formed as Hitler's bodyguard within the army.
March 21	Dachau, the first Nazi concentration camp, is set up. Concentration camps and **labo camps** are set up steadily after this.
April 26	The **Gestapo** (Nazi secret police force) is formed.
July 14	Political parties other than the Nazi Party are banned in Germany.

1934

July 20	The SS is now in charge of their own affairs—they are no longer part of the army.
August 2	Hitler makes himself *Führer*, sole leader of Germany.

1935

September 15	The Nuremberg Laws passed against German Jews.

1937

July 16	Buchenwald concentration camp is set up.

1938

March 13	The German army marches into Austria and the Austrian people vote to become part of Germany again.
August 8	Mauthausen concentration camp is set up.
October 28	The first group of Jews are deported from Poland by the Polish government.
November 9	Synagogues are burned and shops and homes are looted in Nazi-led violence against Jewish people known as *Kristallnacht*.

1939

September 1	Germany invades Poland. Nazis begin to pass laws against Polish Jews restricting the work they can do, as in Germany in 1933–1936. Soviet Union invades Poland from the east on September 17.
September 3	Britain and France declare war on Germany.
September 28	Germany and the Soviet Union split Poland up between them.

1940

February 12	The first group of Jews are forcibly removed from their homes in Germany and taken to **ghettos** in Poland.
April 9	Germany invades Denmark and Norway.
April 27	Himmler is told to build a camp at Auschwitz.
April 30	A large ghetto is set up in the Polish city of Lodz. More ghettos are planned.
May 10	Germany invades Belgium, France, Luxembourg, and the Netherlands.
June 22	France signs armistice with Germany.

1941

April 6	Germany invades Yugoslavia and Greece.
June 22	Germany invades the Soviet Union; mass executions of Jews take place as the German army moves through the Soviet Union.
September 1	All German Jews over the age of six have to wear a yellow Star of David with *"Jude"* ("Jew") in black on it.
From September	Mass gassings at Auschwitz begin with Soviet prisoners-of-war and continue. They focus on Jews and become more regular from January 1942.
October 16	Mass **deportation** of German Jews to Poland begins.
October 28	10,000 Jews are selected and killed at the Kovno ghetto, Poland.
December 7	Japan bombs the American fleet at Pearl Harbor, bringing the U.S. into the war.
December 8	The first gassing of Jews takes place at Chelmno.
December 11	Germany and Italy declare war on the United States.

1942

January 20	Wannsee Conference of leading Nazis outlines the "Final Solution" to what the Nazis call the "Jewish Problem."
March 1	The first group of Jews are deported to Sobibor **death camp.**
March 17	The first group of Jews are deported to Belzec death camp.
March 26	The first Jews are deported to Auschwitz-Birkenau and Majdanek death camps.
March 27	The first French Jews are deported to Auschwitz.
July 15	The first Dutch Jews are deported to Auschwitz.
July 22	Daily deportations to Treblinka from the Warsaw ghetto begin.
October 4	Himmler orders that all Jews in concentration camps are to be sent to Auschwitz-Birkenau to be killed.

1943

April 19	The Warsaw ghetto revolt begins.
June 11	Himmler orders all remaining ghettos to be emptied and their inhabitants killed.

1944

March 23	Deportation of Jews from Greece (occupied by the Germans) begins.
April 9	Two Jews escape from Auschwitz and send news of the camp out of **occupied** Europe to the **Allies**. News of the camp cannot now be ignored.
May 15	Mass deportation and gassing of Hungarian Jews begins.
From June	Death marches from camps in the east begin, as prisoners are marched in front of advancing Soviet troops.
June 6	Allied troops land in Normandy.

1945

17 January	Final death march from Auschwitz-Birkenau takes place.
27 January	Soviet troops reach Auschwitz.
11 April	American troops reach Buchenwald.
15 April	British troops reach Belsen.
29 April	American troops reach Dachau.
30 April	Hitler commits suicide in Berlin, as the city is occupied by Soviet troops.
5 May	American troops reach Mauthausen.
7 May	Germany surrenders.
20 November	The Nuremberg trials of Nazi war criminals begin. The first war criminals are executed in October 1946.

Glossary

Ally country that fought against Nazi Germany in World War II

anti-Semitism being prejudiced against Jewish people

Aryan word used by the Nazis to mean people with northern European ancestors, without any ancestors from what they called "inferior" races, such as Poles, Slavs, or Jews. Aryans were supposed to be blonde, blue-eyed, and sturdy.

camp *See* concentration camp, death camp, and labor camp.

concentration camp prison camp set up by the Nazis under a special law that meant that the prisoners were never tried and were never given a release date. The Nazis could put anyone in these camps, for any reason or none, for as long as they wanted.

crematorium place with special ovens for burning bodies

death camp camp set up by the Nazis to murder as many people, most of them Jewish, as quickly and cheaply as possible. Most of the victims were gassed.

deportation being sent away from a place and not allowed to return

displaced person (DP) camp camp set up after World War II for people who had been taken from their homes and countries and separated from their families. Workers in these camps tried to trace families and help people return home.

Einsatzgruppen special units of the German army set up by the Nazis. These units went into eastern Europe at the same time as the army. Their job was supposedly to round up and kill civilians who were a danger to the Reich. In fact, they were told to kill Jews. *Einsatzkommando 3* was a sub-unit of the *Einsatzgruppen.*

Gestapo secret police set up by the Nazis in 1933

ghetto area of a town or city, walled or fenced off from the rest of the city, where Jewish people were forced to live

guerrilla fighting small groups of people, fighting from hiding, using tactics such as ambush; not open warfare

Gypsy member of a traveling people who speak the Romany language; the Nazis used the word "Gypsy" to describe all traveling or homeless people, or even those whose ancestors had been travelers or homeless

Holocaust huge destruction or sacrifice. When it appears with a capital "H," it refers to the deliberate attempt by the Nazi government in Germany to destroy all of the Jewish people in their power.

Jew (Jewish) someone who follows the Jewish faith. The Nazis also called people Jews if they had Jewish ancestors, even if they had changed their faith.

Judenfrei "Jew free;" a place with no Jewish people living there

Judenrat "Jewish Council;" the people put in charge of the ghettos by the Nazis

kapo prisoner who was put in charge of other prisoners when they were working

Kindertransport name given to the British government's acceptance of about 10,000 Jewish children into Britain from Germany in 1939. These children had to have a home to go to, but they did not need visas, just proof of age and identity.

labor camp prison camp set up by the Nazis that used prisoners as cheap labor

liberation used in this book to mean a place, especially a concentration camp, being freed from the control of the SS. Camps were liberated by Allied soldiers.

Nazi member of the Nazi party. Nazi is short for *Nationalsozialistische Deutsche Arbeiterpartei*, the National Socialist German Workers' Party.

occupied used in this book to mean a country that has been captured by Germany and is ruled by Nazis supported by the German army

papers used in this book to mean all the different documents needed under Nazi rule: identity card, work permit, travel permit, Aryan certificate, and so on

partisan someone who fights an army that has invaded and taken over their country

political having to do with ideas and actions of government; person arrested for opposing Nazi ideas or actions

prisoner functionary prisoner, usually a German criminal, put in charge of other prisoners as a *kapo* or *blockältester*

propaganda information and ideas that are worded and presented so that people will accept and believe them, even if they are not true

rabbi spiritual leader of a Jewish synagogue, who conducts the services and teaches and advises adults and children

race group of people with the same ancestors

Reich empire. *See* Third Reich.

refugee someone fleeing the place they live, usually in fear of their lives

resettlement to take people away from one place and make them settle somewhere else. Jewish people who were moved to the ghettos and then to the camps by the Nazis were promised they would be "resettled" in the east.

resistance name given to groups formed in countries taken over by the Nazis to secretly fight the Nazis and try to drive them out of the country

roll call count of all the prisoners in a camp, usually morning and evening

sabotage to deliberately damage something so it will not work

SS (short for *Schutzstaffel*) security staff. The SS began as Hitler's personal bodyguard. Later, they ran concentration camps and death camps. Everyone in the SS swore loyalty to Hitler, rather than Germany.

swastika equal armed cross with each arm bent at a right angle in a clockwise direction. It was the symbol adopted by the Nazi party.

Third Reich "the third empire." The Nazis saw their rule as the third German empire, with Hitler as the emperor, or *Führer*.

transport used in this book to refer to a trainload of people being sent to the camps

undesirable word used by the Nazis to describe any person that they did not approve of because of political beliefs, race, religion, or behavior

visa written approval made on a passport stating that a person can leave a country

Zionist person who believed in the setting up of a Jewish nation in Palestine

Further Reading

Frank, Anne. *Diary of a Young Girl.* Columbus, Ohio: Prentice Hall, 1993.

Shuter, Jane. *Auschwitz.* Chicago: Heinemann Library, 1999.

Tames, Richard. *Anne Frank.* Chicago: Heinemann Library, 1998.

Tames, Richard. *Adolf Hitler.* Chicago: Heinemann Library, 1998.

Whittock, Martyn. *Hitler & National Socialism.* Chicago: Heinemann Library, 1996.

Wiesel, Elie. *Night.* New York: Bantam Books, 1982.

Willoughby, Susan. *The Holocaust.* Chicago: Heinemann Library, 2000.

Sources

The author and publisher gratefully acknowledge the publications from which written sources in this book are drawn. In some cases, the wording or sentence structure has been simplified to make the material appropriate for a school readership.

Adelsberger, Lucie. *Auschwitz: A Doctor's Story.* Boston: Northeastern University Press, 1995. (pp. 30–31)

Altbeker Cyrus, Ruth. *A Jump For Life.* London: Constable & Robinson Ltd, 1997. (pp. 38–39)

Cohen, Rich. *The Avengers: A Jewish War Story.* Westminster, Md.: Alfred A. Knopf Incorporated, 2000. (pp. 7, 16)

Eliach, Yaffa. *Once There Was a World: A 900 Year Chronicle of the Shtetl of Eishyshok.* New York: Little, Brown and Company, 1998. (pp. 42–43)

Fénelon, Fania. *Playing For Time.* Syracuse, N.Y.: Syracuse University Press, 1997. (pp. 32–35)

Fox, Anne L. *My Heart in a Suitcase.* Portland, Oreg.: Vallentine Mitchell Publishers, 1996. (pp. 8–9)

Gerda and Kurt Klein Foundation, website (pp. 10–11)

Gilbert, Martin. *Never Again: A Story of the Holocaust.* New York: Universe Publishing, 2000. (pp. 40–41)

Gill, Anton. *The Journey Back from Hell: Conversations with Concentration Camp Survivors.* New York: Morrow/Avon, 1994. (pp. 7, 36–37)

Greenfeld, Howard. *The Hidden Children.* Boston: Houghton Mifflin Company, 1993. (pp. 12–15)

Greenman, Leon. *An Englishman in Auschwitz.* Portland, Oreg.: Vallentine Mitchell Publishers, 2001. (pp. 44–45)

Gryn, Hugo. *Chasing Shadows.* East Rutherford, N.J.: Viking Penguin, 2000. (pp. 26–29)

Klein, Gerda Weissmann. *All But My Life.* Reprinted by permission of Hill and Wang (New York), a division of Farrar, Straus and Giroux, LLC. © 1957, 1995 by Gerda Weissmann Klein. (pp. 7, 18–21)

Selvage, Douglas (translator). *Auschwitz: Nazi Death Camp.* Oswiecim, Poland: Auschwitz-Birkenau State Museum, 1998. (pp. 40–41)

Sobolewicz, Tadeusz. *But I Survived.* Oswiecim, Poland: Auschwitz-Birkenau State Museum, 1998. (pp. 7, 22–25)

Places of Interest and Websites

Florida Holocaust Museum
55 Fifth Street South
St. Petersburg, FL 33701
Visitor information: (727) 820-0100
Website: *http://www.flholocaustmuseum.org*

Holocaust Memorial Center
6602 West Maple Road
West Bloomfield, MI 48322
Visitor information: (248) 661-0840
Website: *http://holocaustcenter.org*

Holocaust Museum Houston
5401 Caroline Street
Houston, TX 77004
Visitor information: (713) 942-8000
Website: *http://www.hmh.org*

Simon Wiesenthal Center: Museum of Tolerance
Simon Wiesenthal Plaza
9786 West Pico Blvd.
Los Angeles, CA 90035
Visitor information: (310) 553-8403
Website: *http://www.museumoftolerance.com*

United States Holocaust Memorial Museum
100 Raoul Wallenberg Place, SW
Washington, D.C. 20024
Visitor information: (202) 488-0400
Website: *http://www.ushmm.org*

Website warning

1. Almost all Holocaust websites have been designed for adult users. They may contain horrifying and upsetting information and pictures.
2. Some people wish to minimize the Holocaust, or even deny that it happened at all. Some of their websites pretend to be delivering unbiased facts and information. To be sure of getting accurate information, it is always best to use an officially recognized site such as the ones listed on this page.
3. If you plan to visit a Holocaust website, ask an adult to view the site with you.

Index

Adelsberger, Lucie 30–31
anti-semitism 7, 48
Aryan race 4
Auschwitz 9, 10, 21, 22–24, 25
Auschwitz-Birkenau 27, 31, 32–35, 37, 40, 45

barracks 20, 30, 31
brutality 22, 23, 24, 25, 28
Buchenwald 6, 24, 45, 46

camp food 23, 24
chances of survival 6, 7, 32, 33, 42
children 8–9, 12–13
Cohen, Elie 7, 36–37, 49
collaboration 36, 37, 49
concentration camps 20, 29
Cyrus, Ruth 38–39
Czechoslovakia 4, 5, 26

Dachau 4
death camps 5, 18, 20, 26, 32
death marches 21, 25, 28, 29, 31, 45
Denmark 42
deportations 19, 26, 30, 41, 45
displaced persons (DP) camps 15, 25, 43
doctors 30, 31, 36–37

Einsatzgruppen 42
emigration 10
escapes 39, 40–41

feelings and emotions of the survivors 6, 9, 13, 37, 46–49
Fenelon, Fania 32–35, 48
Fox, Anne 8–9

gas chambers 27, 32
Gestapo 30, 36, 42
ghettos 14, 16, 17, 19, 20, 26, 38
Goldstein, Rosette 12–13
Greenman, Leon 44–45
Gryn, Hugo 26–29
guerrilla fighting 17
guilt, feelings of 6, 49
Gypsies 5, 31

hiding 12–13, 14, 15, 36, 38, 43
Hitler, Adolf 4, 25, 49
Holocaust 5, 6, 9, 13, 14, 21, 25
hope 6, 7, 35

Jewish Council 41
Jewish people 5, 6, 7, 8–9, 10, 11, 12, 13, 14–15, 16, 17, 18–19, 22, 23, 26, 30, 41, 42–43, 44, 48
jobs 32
Judenrat 30

kapos 33
Kindertransports 8
Klein, Kurt 10–11, 21
Korczak, Ruzka 16–17
Kovner, Abba 7, 16, 17
Kristallnacht 10

labor camps 11, 20–21, 36
Levi, Primo 7, 47, 49
liberation 6, 7, 15, 17, 21, 29, 31, 35, 45, 46
Lithuania 14–15, 42–43

medical experiments 37
Michaelowski, Zvi 43

Nazi propaganda 7, 12, 47
Nazis 4–5, 7, 8, 10, 11, 14, 18, 22, 26, 30, 35, 44
Netherlands 36, 44–45

orchestras and music 33–34, 35

partisans 7, 10, 16, 17, 25, 38, 41, 43
Poland 5, 7, 16–17, 18, 38, 48
political prisoners 4, 5, 22
Polofsky, Zelda 14–15
prisoner functionaries 22
prisoner numbers 22, 33
processing arrivals 22

racial theories 4, 5, 22
religious faith 6, 7
resistance movements 10, 17, 22, 32, 38, 40

Schindler, Oskar 47
shoes and uniforms 7, 22, 31, 33
sick prisoners 21, 23, 24, 31
Sobolewicz, Tadeusz 7, 22–25
SS 4, 19, 20, 22, 25, 31, 32, 34, 36, 40
support, mutual 6, 7, 21

Terezín 9
transports 9, 26–27, 30, 32, 36, 39

Vrba, Rudolf 40–41

Wiesel, Elie 46
Weissmann Klein, Gerda 7, 11, 18–21
Wetzler, Alfred 40–41
Wiesenthal, Simon 49

Zionists 16, 17